My Fun with shapes Book

by
Fedelia Grandison
illustrated
by
Mshindo I

EWORLD INC.

Buffalo, New York
14209
eeworldinc@yahoo.com

Shapes are fun when you learn each one
So let us begin and have some fun
All the shapes together
One by one

square

A square has four sides
All the same size
Like a gift box tied up with string
Alphabet blocks
carried by toy trucks
To build just about anything

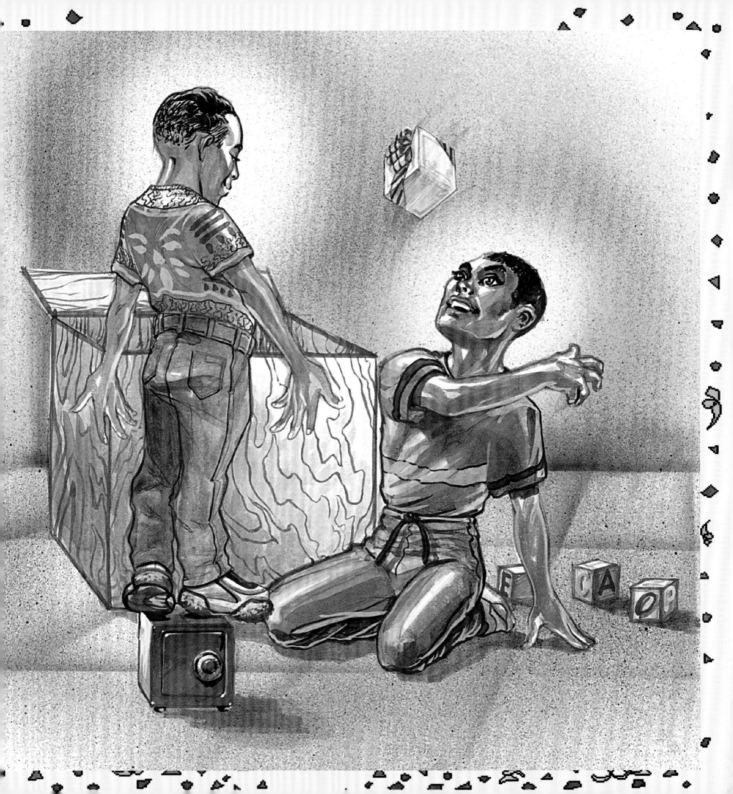

Now let us look at a circle

circle

Circles are bubbles floating free
A circle is like an orange up in a tree
A bouncing ball
Balloons floating free
in the sky
up, up, up and away they fly

Now let us look at a ring

A ring is a circle
with a hole in the middle
Like a hoopla hoop
that spins when you wiggle

Now let us look at a heart shape

heart

Hearts say hugs and lots of love
Pink ones, red ones, yellow ones too
A heart shaped gift
from me to you

Now let us look at a diamond shape

diamond

A kite up in the sky
is a diamond flying high
Here's a diamond for you to treasure
A diamond ring will last forever

Now let us look at a rectangle shape

rectangle

A rectangle has four sides
Two sides are long
And two sides are short
Like a picture on the wall
Like a window or a door
Can you find any more ?

Now let us look at a crescent

crescent

Crescents are not often seen
They are rare indeed
But the moon up in the sky
Is a crescent shape way up high

Now let us look at a triangle

triangle

Triangles have three sides
Like an airplane wing or a pyramid
A boat's sail and
the flap of an envelope you mail

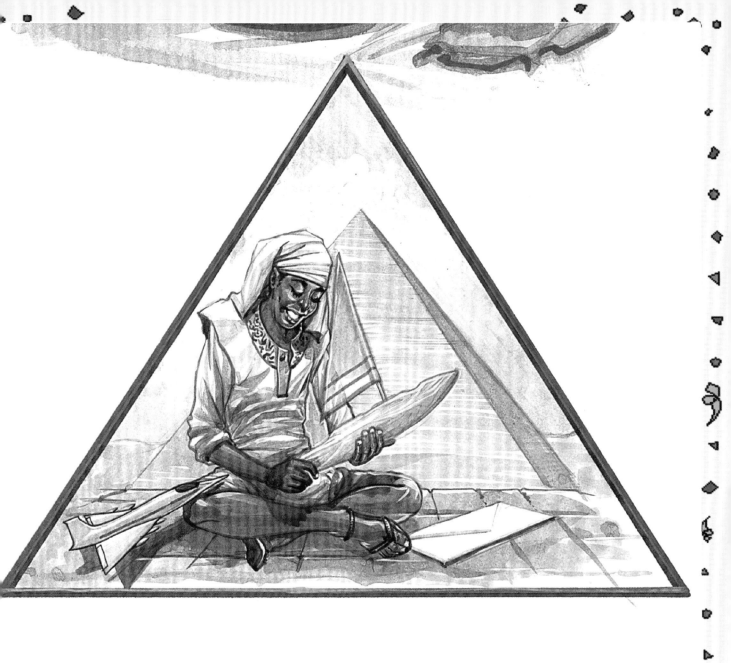

Now let us look at an oval

Ovals are round and a bit long
An egg is a perfect one
Here is a cat wearing a hat
Sleeping on an oval mat

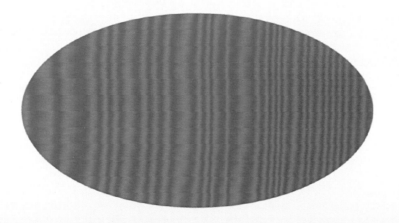

Now let us look at a star

star

A fairy's wand to make a wish
on a big bright star
It shines so bright
All through the night
Up in the sky so far

All the shapes together
Building things forever
Some big and some small
Look around the picture
The shapes are close together
Can you find them all ?

Our Books Make Excellent Gifts

Children Titles

Come To My Island	R Donovan	$ 7.95
Daily Prayers & Meditation	Hafeesa Nettles	$ 7.95
When I Look In The Mirror	Sopoeia Greywolf	$ 6.95
Melanin and Me	Beverly Crespo	$ 7.95
The Path	Michael Markman	$ 8.95
Grandma's ABC's of Fruits & Vegetables	Beverly Ballard	$ 5.95
Nandi's Magic Garden	Ron Matthews	$ 8.95
Little Zeng's ABC's	Chris Hall	$ 4.95
Afro-Tots Numbers	O Gift	$ 3.95
Afro-Tots Letters	O Gift	$ 3.95

Fun with Series

Fun with Numbers 123	F Grandison	$ 3.95
Fun with Letters A B C	S Williamson	$ 3.95
Fun with Shapes	F Grandison	$ 3.95
Fun with Colors	F Grandison	$ 3.95
Adventure Fun with Numbers		$ 2.95
Adventure Fun with Shapes & Colors		$ 2.95
Adventure Fun with Letters		$ 2.95

Coloring & Activity Books

When I Look In The Mirror Coloring & Activity	$ 2.95
Little Zeng Goes To Harlem	$ 2.95
Little Zeng's Ancient Egypt	$ 2.95
Little Zeng Hannibal	$ 2.95
Little Zeng	$ 2.95

Please send for our complete catalog

EWORLD INC.

Buffalo, New York
14209
eeworldinc@yahoo.com